My Daddy's HEART is Purple

KARL PORFIRIO

ISBN 978-1-64003-534-8 (Hardcover)
ISBN 978-1-64003-535-5 (Digital)

Covenant Books, Inc.
11661 Hwy 707
Murrells Inlet, SC 29576
www.covenantbooks.com

To my grandson

Landon,

who I love infinity

times a million!

One day I was riding in the car with my nonno. In case you don't know, that means "grandpa" in Italian.

We stopped at a red light. I was looking out my window, and I saw the car next to us. It had a sticker on the back of the car. The words said "Purple Heart," and there was a picture of a heart too.

"Nonno," I asked, "there is a sticker on this car, and it says Purple Heart. There is also a picture of a face on the heart. What is it for?"

"Well, I'm so glad you saw this, little one, and I am even more glad you asked about it," said Nonno. "You see, a Purple Heart is very, very special."

"It is? How come?" I asked.

"Well, you see, this is a very special award," Nonno said.

"Award?" I asked. "What do you mean?"

Then Nonno said, "You know how when you do something good at your school, the teacher puts a gold star or a smiley face on your chart? That's a type of award that lets you and everyone who sees it know you did something special."

"Ohhh," I said.

"Let me tell you a story now, little one, so listen, okay?" Nonno's voice got very serious. "Before you were born, your father was in the Air Force. Do you remember me talking to you about that?"

"A little," I said.

"When a person in the military does something extra special, they receive awards or medals. The Purple Heart is one of those medals," he said. "The person's face on the medal is General George Washington."

"You mean the first president that is on our money? That George Washington?" I asked.

"Yes, that George Washington," Nonno said. "He wanted to give a special medal to those that earned one during their military service. Do you understand?" Nonno asked.

"Yes, I think I do, Nonno," I said.

"That's good," Nonno said. "So when you were just a little bitty baby, your daddy had to go far away to help protect America. While he was doing his job, he was injured very badly."

"Is that why he had to go to heaven and be with the angels, Nonno?" I saw a tear coming out of his eye, and I said, "Are you crying, Nonno? Please don't cry."

Nonno said, "Oh, I am not crying."

But I saw him wipe away the tear with his finger.

Then Nonno said, "I miss your daddy very much, but I am very, very proud of him! He is an American hero, and he served his country well, just like many other brave men and women do."

"Is my daddy's heart purple?" I asked.

Nonno laughed a little. "Yes, your daddy does have a Purple Heart," he said.

"Well then, I am very proud of my daddy too," I said.

"Good," said Nonno. "You should be very proud."

Just then I noticed Nonno was turning into our favorite ice cream place. He parked the car then helped me out of it.

We both went into the store.

"You want your usual?" Nonno asked me.

"No, Nonno, I think today I will get what you always get."

Nonno smiled at me a great big smile. Then he said to the clerk, "Two red, white, and blue rocket pops, please."

"I love you, Nonno," I said.

"I love you more, little one!"

In loving memory

My son, my hero

Senior Airman Tre Porfirio

ABOUT THE AUTHOR

Karl Porfirio, also known as Nonno, is a devoted father and grandfather. He is formerly from Tennessee, the beach in Florida, and now resides in the peaceful mountains of North Georgia.

You can e-mail him at karl.porfirio@gmail.com.

CPSIA information can be obtained
at www.ICGtesting.com
Printed in the USA
LVHW07*1922160718
583905LV00019B/449/P